NORWAY CRUISE GUIDE 2025

Norway by Sea: A Complete 2025 Guide to Fjords, Glaciers & Coastal Wonders.

COLE WINCHESTER

Copyright

© 2025 [Cole Winchester]. All rights reserved.

No part of this publication may be copied, distributed, or reproduced in any form, whether through printing, recording, electronic transmission, or mechanical duplication, without prior written consent from the publisher. Limited exceptions apply for brief excerpts used in reviews or non-commercial purposes that comply with applicable copyright laws.

NORWAY CRUISE GUIDE 2025

NORWAY CRUISE GUIDE 2025

NORWAY CRUISE GUIDE 2025

TABLE OF CONTENTS

INTRODUCTION 8
  Welcome to the Land of the Fjords 8
  Why Choose a Norway Cruise? 9
  Best Time to Cruise Norway 14
  How to Use This Guide 15

PLANNING YOUR CRUISE 16
  Choosing the Right Cruise Line & Ship 16
  Budgeting for a Norway Cruise 18
  Packing Essentials for Arctic & Fjord Adventures 20
  Understanding Norway's Cruise Regions 22

UNDERSTANDING NORWAY'S CRUISE REGIONS 24
  Southern Norway: Coastal Charms & Historic Towns 24
  Western Fjords: Iconic Waterways & Natural Wonders 27
  Arctic Norway: Northern Lights & Midnight Sun 29
  Svalbard & Beyond: The Edge of the Arctic 31

TOP NORWEGIAN CRUISE PORTS 33
  Bergen – The Gateway to the Fjords 33
  Geiranger – The Jewel of the Fjords 35
  Flåm – A Scenic Railway Paradise 36
  Ålesund – The Art Nouveau City 37
  Tromsø – The Arctic Capital 39
  Honningsvåg – Gateway to the North Cape 40

NORWEGIAN FJORDS – THE HEART OF THE CRUISE 42
  What Makes Norway's Fjords So Special? 42

NORWAY CRUISE GUIDE 2025

Geirangerfjord – Norway's Most Iconic Fjord 43

Sognefjord – The King of the Fjords 44

Hardangerfjord – The Orchard of Norway 45

Nærøyfjord – The Narrow Wonder 46

Lysefjord – Home of Pulpit Rock 47

Wildlife & Nature in the Fjords 48

SHORE EXCURSIONS & ACTIVITIES 50

Must-Try Fjord Boat Tours & Kayaking Adventures 50

Scenic Railway Journeys 52

Hiking Norway's Most Famous Trails 54

Sami Culture & Reindeer Encounters in the Arctic 55

Wildlife Safaris & Whale Watching 56

Arctic Circle Adventures: Dog Sledding & Snowmobiling 57

ONBOARD CRUISE EXPERIENCE 58

What to Expect on a Norway Cruise Ship 58

Dining & Norwegian Cuisine Onboard 60

Entertainment & Enrichment Programs 62

Wellness & Relaxation: Spas, Pools & Outdoor Hot Tubs 63

Northern Lights Viewing & Midnight Sun Experiences 64

NORWAY'S RICH CULTURE & TRADITIONS 67

Viking Heritage & History 67

Norwegian Festivals & Celebrations 69

Sami Indigenous Culture & Arctic Traditions 70

The Scandinavian Lifestyle: "Kos" & Outdoor Living 73

PRACTICAL TRAVEL TIPS & ESSENTIALS 76

NORWAY CRUISE GUIDE 2025

Norwegian Currency, Costs & Payment Methods 76
Language Tips & Common Norwegian Phrases 78
Internet & Connectivity at Sea 80
Travel Insurance & Health Precautions 81
Sustainable & Responsible Travel in Norway 82

SPECIAL INTEREST CRUISES & UNIQUE EXPERIENCES 85

Northern Lights Winter Cruises 85
Midnight Sun Summer Voyages 87
Expedition Cruises to Svalbard & the Arctic 89
Photography Cruises: Capturing the Fjords & Arctic Wonders .. 91
Luxury & Small Ship Cruises vs. Large Cruise Lines 92

NORWAY CRUISE FAQS & TROUBLESHOOTING 94

What If the Weather Changes? 94
How to Handle Seasickness in Norwegian Waters? 96
What Should I Do If My Luggage Is Lost? 99
How Can I Stay Connected With Family While Cruising? 101

RESOURCES & FINAL THOUGHTS 103

Recommended Books & Travel Guides 103
Useful Apps & Websites for Norway Travel 105
Packing Checklist & Last-Minute Essentials 107
Final Words: Making the Most of Your Norway Cruise 109

INTRODUCTION

Welcome to the Land of the Fjords

Picture yourself gliding through mirror-like waters, surrounded by towering cliffs draped in waterfalls that cascade down into deep, mystical fjords. Snow-capped peaks reflect on the still water, while the crisp, invigorating air fills your lungs. Welcome to Norway—the land of breathtaking landscapes, Viking heritage, and natural wonders that seem almost otherworldly.

A Norway cruise is unlike any other travel experience. It is a journey into the heart of nature's raw beauty, where every turn reveals a new vista more stunning than the last. Whether you are chasing the Northern Lights in the Arctic Circle, exploring charming coastal villages with colorful wooden houses, or soaking in the serenity of the fjords, a cruise through Norway is an adventure that stays with you forever.

But what makes a Norwegian cruise so special? Unlike traditional ocean cruises that focus on sun-soaked beaches and tropical escapes, Norway offers a completely different kind of voyage—one that is defined by dramatic landscapes, untouched wilderness, and a rich cultural history. Cruising is the best way to explore Norway's rugged coastline, which is dotted with thousands of islands, deep fjords, and picturesque fishing villages that are often only accessible by sea.

From the moment you set sail, you'll be transported into a world were nature reigns supreme. You might spot a pod of orcas slicing through the icy waters, witness the midnight sun casting a golden glow over the horizon, or marvel at the sight of reindeer grazing under the vast Arctic sky. Every day brings a new adventure, a new discovery, and a new story to tell.

Why Choose a Norway Cruise?

Cruising in Norway offers a perfect blend of luxury and adventure. Unlike road trips or rail journeys, a cruise allows you to visit multiple destinations without the hassle of packing and unpacking. You wake up in a new, stunning location every day while enjoying the comfort of a world-class ship.

Here are some key reasons why a Norway cruise is the ultimate way to explore this Scandinavian wonderland:

Unmatched Scenic Beauty

Norway's fjords are among the most spectacular natural wonders on Earth. Carved by glaciers over thousands of years, these deep, narrow waterways create a mesmerizing landscape of steep cliffs, emerald-green waters, and lush valleys. The most famous fjords—Geirangerfjord, Sognefjord, and Nærøyfjord—are UNESCO-listed sites that are best experienced by boat.

A cruise offers front-row seats to these breathtaking vistas, allowing you to witness their grandeur from the perfect vantage point—the deck of your ship. Whether bathed in summer's golden light or dusted with winter snow, the fjords never fail to leave travelers in awe.

The Midnight Sun & Northern Lights

Depending on when you travel, a Norwegian cruise offers two of the world's most extraordinary natural phenomena: the Midnight Sun and the Northern Lights.

Summer Cruises (Midnight Sun): If you sail between late May and late July, you'll experience endless daylight in Norway's northern regions. The sun never sets, casting a surreal glow over the landscape and allowing for longer exploration hours. This phenomenon is particularly magical in places like Tromsø, the Lofoten Islands, and the North Cape.

Winter Cruises (Northern Lights): From September to March, the Arctic sky comes alive with the ethereal dance of the Aurora Borealis. A cruise along Norway's northern coast, especially around Tromsø and Alta, offers one of the best chances to witness this breathtaking display. Imagine standing on the deck of your ship, wrapped in a warm blanket, watching vibrant green and purple lights swirl across the night sky—an experience that words can barely capture.

A Journey Through History & Culture

Norway's past is deeply intertwined with the legendary Viking Age. As you cruise along the coast, you'll have opportunities to visit ancient Viking settlements, world-class museums, and historic towns that tell the story of this seafaring nation.

In cities like **Bergen**, you can walk through the iconic Bryggen Wharf, a UNESCO-listed site that once served as a hub for the Hanseatic League's trading empire. In **Trondheim**, visit the magnificent Nidaros Cathedral, a medieval masterpiece that has been a pilgrimage site for centuries. And in **Oslo**, Norway's vibrant capital, explore the Viking Ship Museum, home to incredibly well-preserved longships from over a thousand years ago.

Beyond the Vikings, Norway is a country rich in folklore, myths, and traditions. From the mysterious tales of trolls lurking in the mountains to the colorful Sami culture in the Arctic north, every region has its own unique stories to share.

Adventure at Every Turn

For those who crave adventure, a Norway cruise is an absolute paradise. The country's rugged terrain offers countless opportunities for outdoor activities.

Hiking: Some of the world's most famous hiking trails are accessible from cruise ports. If your itinerary includes **Stavanger**, you can embark on a trek to **Pulpit Rock (Preikestolen)**, an awe-inspiring cliff that rises 604 meters above Lysefjord. From **Geiranger**, you can hike to **Flydalsjuvet**, a stunning viewpoint that offers a panoramic vista of the fjord below.

Kayaking & Boat Excursions: Exploring the fjords by kayak allows you to get up close to waterfalls, wildlife, and untouched nature. Many cruises offer kayaking excursions in places like **Flåm**, where you can paddle through the calm waters of Aurlandsfjord.

Wildlife Encounters: Norway's diverse ecosystems are home to a variety of fascinating wildlife. Keep your eyes peeled for **whales**, **puffins**, **sea eagles**, and even **polar bears** if your cruise ventures as far as Svalbard.

Dog Sledding & Snowmobiling: If you're cruising in winter, don't miss the chance to experience the Arctic wilderness on a dog sled or snowmobile. Tours in places like Tromsø and Alta offer thrilling rides through snowy landscapes.

Best Time to Cruise Norway

Norway's cruise season runs from **April to September**, with each month offering a unique experience:

Spring (April-May): Fewer crowds, melting snow, and waterfalls at their most powerful. Perfect for nature lovers who want to see the fjords in full bloom.

Summer (June-August): The peak season, offering the warmest weather, longest daylight hours, and the chance to experience the Midnight Sun. Ideal for first-time visitors.

Autumn (September-October): Stunning fall foliage, fewer tourists, and the beginning of Northern Lights season.

Winter (November-March): For those who want to chase the Northern Lights, embark on an Arctic adventure, or experience Norway's festive Christmas markets.

How to Use This Guide

This guide is designed to help you plan the perfect Norwegian cruise. Whether you're a first-time cruiser or a seasoned traveler, you'll find valuable insights, practical tips, and in-depth destination highlights to make the most of your journey.

Each chapter covers essential aspects of cruising in Norway—from choosing the right itinerary and understanding the best ports of call to experiencing local culture and finding hidden gems beyond the tourist hotspots. You'll also get expert recommendations on shore excursions, dining experiences, and must-see natural wonders.

No matter which routes you choose, one thing is certain: a Norway cruise is a voyage unlike any other. It's a journey of wonder, adventure, and pure magic—where every moment feels like stepping into a postcard.

So, get ready to set sail and explore the breathtaking beauty of Norway!

PLANNING YOUR CRUISE

Choosing the Right Cruise Line & Ship

Selecting the perfect cruise line is the first and most important step in planning your Norwegian adventure. While many major cruise lines offer itineraries through Norway's fjords and Arctic regions, they vary greatly in terms of luxury, amenities, onboard experiences, and the type of traveler they cater to.

Large vs. Small Cruise Ships

One of the biggest decisions you'll need to make is whether to sail on a **large ocean liner** or a **smaller, expedition-style ship**. Each has its own advantages:

Large Cruise Ships (1,500+ passengers)

Offer extensive onboard entertainment, restaurants, spas, and large cabins.

Ideal for families, first-time cruisers, and those who enjoy a resort-like experience.

Limited access to smaller, remote ports due to size.

Examples: Royal Caribbean, MSC, Celebrity Cruises.

Small & Expedition Ships (50–1,500 passengers)

Provide a more intimate experience, often with expert guides and lecturers onboard.

Can dock at smaller ports and sail deeper into fjords that larger ships cannot access.

Best for nature lovers, photographers, and adventure seekers.

Examples: Hurtigruten, Viking Cruises, Ponant, Silversea.

If you're looking for a more immersive and adventurous experience, **Hurtigruten** is one of the best choices. This Norwegian company operates both classic coastal voyages and expedition cruises that take you into the Arctic Circle and beyond.

Cruise Length & Itineraries

Norway cruises range from **short 5-day fjord getaways** to **two-week Arctic expeditions**. Your choice will depend on your interests, budget, and available time.

Short Fjord Cruises (5–7 days): Perfect for those who want to explore the highlights of western Norway's fjords. Typical departure points include **Bergen, Copenhagen, or Amsterdam**.

Classic Norwegian Coastline Cruises (10–14 days): These cover a longer stretch of Norway's coast, including famous ports like **Geiranger, Ålesund, Tromsø, and Honningsvåg (North Cape)**.

Arctic & Svalbard Cruises (12+ days): For travelers who want to venture into the remote Arctic regions, these cruises sail beyond mainland Norway to **Svalbard, Greenland, and sometimes even Iceland**.

Budgeting for a Norway Cruise

Norway is one of the most expensive travel destinations in the world, so careful budgeting is essential. The cost of your cruise will depend on the cruise line, time of year, cabin type, and extra excursions.

Key Expenses to Consider

Cruise Fare: Prices vary significantly based on the season. Expect to pay between **$1,000–$5,000 per person**

for a 7-day cruise. Luxury lines or expedition cruises can cost **$6,000+ per person**.

Flights: Round-trip flights to Norway from the U.S. or Europe can range from **$500–$2,000**, depending on the season.

Shore Excursions: While some hikes and scenic walks are free, guided excursions (e.g., kayaking, dog sledding, or the Flåm Railway) can cost **$100–$300 per person**.

Food & Drinks: On luxury cruises, food is included, but many mid-range lines charge extra for specialty dining and alcohol. Expect **$10–$15 per cocktail** and **$50–$100 per specialty meal**.

Tips & Gratuities: Some cruise lines include gratuities, while others charge an additional **$10–$20 per day per guest**.

Travel Insurance: Highly recommended, especially for Arctic cruises. Expect to pay **$100–$300 per person** for coverage.

Money-Saving Tips:

Book early to secure lower fares (Norway cruises often sell out a year in advance).

Travel in the shoulder season (April-May or September-October) for better deals.

Look for repositioning cruises that move ships between seasons and offer discounted fares.

Choose a cabin with fewer amenities (e.g., an interior cabin) if you plan to spend most of your time exploring.

Packing Essentials for Arctic & Fjord Adventures

Norwegian weather is famously unpredictable, so packing smart is crucial. No matter when you travel, layering is key.

Clothing Essentials

Base Layers: Moisture-wicking shirts and thermal underwear.

Mid Layers: Fleece or wool sweaters for warmth.

Outer Layers: Waterproof and windproof jackets. A down jacket is a must for Arctic cruises.

Pants: Waterproof hiking pants for outdoor excursions.

Shoes: Comfortable walking shoes and insulated, waterproof boots.

Gloves, Hat & Scarf: Essential, even in summer, especially in the Arctic.

Other Must-Haves

Binoculars: To spot whales, seabirds, and stunning landscapes.

Camera: A DSLR or mirrorless camera with a zoom lens for capturing fjords and wildlife.

Reusable Water Bottle: Tap water in Norway is among the cleanest in the world.

Seasickness Medication: The North Sea can be rough, so it's best to be prepared.

Swimsuit: For onboard hot tubs or thermal pools in Norwegian ports.

Understanding Norway's Cruise Regions

Norway's diverse landscapes make every region unique. Your itinerary will likely cover one or more of the following areas:

Southern Norway: Coastal Charms & Historic Towns

Includes **Oslo, Kristiansand, Arendal, and Stavanger**.

Features charming coastal towns, white sandy beaches, and Viking history.

Best for cultural experiences and mild summer weather.

Western Fjords: Iconic Waterways & Natural Wonders

Includes **Bergen, Flåm, Geiranger, Ålesund, and Stavanger**.

Home to Norway's most famous fjords, including **Geirangerfjord, Sognefjord, and Hardangerfjord**.

Best for dramatic landscapes, scenic train rides, and outdoor adventures.

Arctic Norway: Northern Lights & Midnight Sun

Includes **Tromsø, Alta, Honningsvåg (North Cape), and Kirkenes**.

Best for winter Northern Lights cruises or summer Midnight Sun voyages.

Features Arctic wildlife, Sami culture, and adventure sports like dog sledding.

Svalbard & Beyond: The Edge of the Arctic

Includes **Longyearbyen (Svalbard), Greenland, and sometimes Iceland**.

Home to polar bears, glaciers, and some of the most remote landscapes on Earth.

Best for expedition-style cruises and extreme Arctic experiences.

UNDERSTANDING NORWAY'S CRUISE REGIONS

Norway is one of the most spectacular cruise destinations in the world, offering a wide variety of landscapes, climates, and cultural experiences. Whether you're sailing through the dramatic fjords of the west, exploring the Arctic wilderness of the north, or visiting the picturesque coastal towns of the south, every region has something unique to offer.

Understanding Norway's different cruise regions will help you decide which itinerary best suits your interests. Some travelers prefer the classic fjord experience, while others dream of witnessing the Northern Lights or venturing into the remote Arctic. In this chapter, we'll break down the main cruise regions, highlighting what makes each one special, what to expect, and the must-see destinations along the way.

Southern Norway: Coastal Charms & Historic Towns

What Makes Southern Norway Special?

Southern Norway is known for its charming coastal towns, white wooden houses, and rich Viking history. Unlike the dramatic fjords of the west or the rugged wilderness of the north, this region offers a gentler, more idyllic experience. It is also home to Norway's capital, Oslo, a vibrant city that blends history, modern architecture, and cultural attractions.

If you're looking for a relaxed introduction to Norway with scenic coastal landscapes, historic sites, and pleasant summer weather, Southern Norway is a great choice.

Key Ports & Highlights

Oslo – Norway's Capital of Culture

Visit the **Viking Ship Museum**, home to remarkably well-preserved Viking longships.

Explore **Akershus Fortress**, a medieval castle offering panoramic views of the Oslo Fjord.

Walk along the modern **Aker Brygge** waterfront, filled with restaurants, shops, and museums.

Visit the famous **Vigeland Sculpture Park**, featuring over 200 unique sculptures.

Kristiansand – Norway's Summer Retreat

Stroll through **Posebyen**, the old town district lined with charming white wooden houses.

Relax on **Bystranda Beach**, one of Norway's few sandy beaches.

Visit **Kristiansand Zoo and Amusement Park**, a great stop for families.

Arendal – The Venice of Norway

Explore the **Tyholmen district**, featuring well-preserved 17th-century wooden houses.

Take a boat tour through the beautiful archipelago of islands surrounding the town.

Visit **Merdø**, a historic fishing island with scenic trails and a small museum.

Western Fjords: Iconic Waterways & Natural Wonders

What Makes the Fjords Special?

Norway's western fjords are the crown jewels of the country's natural beauty. These deep, glacially carved waterways are surrounded by towering cliffs, cascading waterfalls, and lush green valleys. Some of the fjords, like **Geirangerfjord and Nærøyfjord**, are UNESCO World Heritage Sites due to their extraordinary landscapes.

This region is perfect for travelers who want to experience Norway's most famous scenery, whether by boat, train, or hiking trail.

Key Fjords & Highlights

Bergen – The Gateway to the Fjords

Walk through **Bryggen Wharf**, a UNESCO-listed Hanseatic trading port.

Ride the **Fløibanen Funicular** to the top of Mount Fløyen for incredible views.

Visit the **Fish Market**, where you can try fresh Norwegian seafood.

Geiranger – The Jewel of the Fjords

Sail through the stunning **Geirangerfjord**, one of the **most famous fjords in the world.**

See the **Seven Sisters Waterfall**, a spectacular set of cascading falls.

Drive the **Eagle Road** or **Dalsnibba Skywalk** for panoramic views of the fjord.

Flåm – Home of the Scenic Railway

Ride the **Flåm Railway**, one of the most scenic train journeys in the world.

Take a boat cruise through **Nærøyfjord**, one of the narrowest fjords in Norway.

Hike or bike along the **Rallarvegen Trail**, a stunning mountain route.

Stavanger – Pulpit Rock & Viking Heritage

Hike to **Preikestolen (Pulpit Rock)**, a breathtaking cliff rising 604 meters above Lysefjord.

Visit the **Norwegian Petroleum Museum**, which explores Norway's offshore oil industry.

Stroll through **Gamle Stavanger**, a beautifully preserved old town with cobblestone streets.

Arctic Norway: Northern Lights & Midnight Sun

What Makes Arctic Norway Special?

As you sail north of the Arctic Circle, the landscapes become more remote, rugged, and wild. This is where you can experience the **Northern Lights in winter** and the **Midnight Sun in summer**. The Arctic region is also home to indigenous Sami culture, rich wildlife, and dramatic mountain landscapes.

If you're looking for adventure, Arctic Norway offers some of the most thrilling experiences, from dog sledding to whale watching.

Key Ports & Highlights

Tromsø – The Arctic Capital

Visit the **Arctic Cathedral**, an architectural masterpiece.

Take the **Fjellheisen Cable Car** for stunning views over Tromsø.

Go on a **Northern Lights tour** in winter or experience **dog sledding**.

Honningsvåg – Gateway to the North Cape

Visit **Nordkapp (North Cape)**, the northernmost point of mainland Europe.

Experience the **Midnight Sun**, where the sun doesn't set for weeks in summer.

Learn about Arctic wildlife at the **North Cape Museum**.

Alta – The City of the Northern Lights

Visit the **Alta Museum**, home to prehistoric rock carvings.

Stay in the **Sorrisniva Igloo Hotel**, a hotel built entirely of ice and snow.

Experience a **Sami cultural tour**, including traditional music and reindeer sledding.

Svalbard & Beyond: The Edge of the Arctic
What Makes Svalbard Special?

Svalbard is one of the northernmost inhabited places on Earth, located halfway between mainland Norway and the North Pole. It is a land of glaciers, polar bears, and untouched Arctic wilderness. Unlike the mainland, which has a mix of cruise options, Svalbard is only accessible through **expedition cruises** that specialize in Arctic exploration.

Key Destinations & Highlights

Longyearbyen – The Capital of Svalbard

Visit the **Svalbard Museum**, which showcases the region's history and wildlife.

Take a **glacier cruise** to see massive ice formations up close.

Explore abandoned Soviet mining towns like **Pyramiden**.

Wildlife & Nature Experiences

Polar Bear Spotting: Svalbard is one of the best places in the world to see wild polar bears.

Glacier Walks & Ice Caves: Guided tours allow you to explore the frozen landscapes.

Whale Watching: The cold Arctic waters are home to blue whales, belugas, and narwhals.

TOP NORWEGIAN CRUISE PORTS

One of the greatest joys of cruising through Norway is the opportunity to visit its breathtaking ports. Each stop offers a unique blend of stunning landscapes, fascinating history, and immersive cultural experiences. From the UNESCO-listed Bryggen Wharf in Bergen to the majestic waterfalls of Geirangerfjord, every port has something extraordinary to offer.

This chapter will take you through Norway's most remarkable cruise ports, detailing their highlights, hidden gems, and must-do activities. Whether you're an adventurer, history enthusiast, or nature lover, these ports will make your Norwegian cruise truly unforgettable.

Bergen – The Gateway to the Fjords

Bergen is often the first stop on a Norwegian cruise and serves as the perfect introduction to the country's natural beauty and cultural heritage. Surrounded by mountains and fjords, this vibrant city is a harmonious blend of history, nature, and modern charm.

Top Attractions & Activities

Bryggen Wharf – A UNESCO World Heritage Site, this historic Hanseatic district is famous for its colorful wooden buildings and fascinating maritime history. Strolling through the narrow alleyways, you'll find boutique shops, art galleries, and traditional restaurants.

Fløibanen Funicular – Take this scenic ride up to **Mount Fløyen** for spectacular panoramic views of Bergen and the surrounding fjords. If you enjoy hiking, there are several trails leading back down to the city.

Fish Market – A must-visit for seafood lovers, this bustling market offers everything from fresh salmon and shrimp to king crab. Try a traditional Norwegian fish soup or a seafood platter while enjoying views of the harbor.

Troldhaugen – The former home of composer Edvard Grieg, this museum offers insight into Norway's musical heritage and features live piano performances.

Hidden Gem: Fantoft Stave Church

A reconstructed 12th-century wooden church located in a serene forest, offering a glimpse into Norway's medieval past.

Geiranger – The Jewel of the Fjords

If there's one port that truly encapsulates Norway's dramatic beauty, it's **Geiranger**. Nestled at the end of the UNESCO-listed **Geirangerfjord**, this tiny village is surrounded by towering cliffs, cascading waterfalls, and lush green valleys.

Top Attractions & Activities

Geirangerfjord Cruise – Sail past breathtaking waterfalls, including the **Seven Sisters** and **The Suitor**, which cascade down the fjord's steep cliffs.

Dalsnibba Skywalk – One of Europe's highest viewpoints accessible by road, offering jaw-dropping panoramic views over Geirangerfjord and the surrounding peaks.

Eagle Road – A winding mountain road with 11 hairpin bends leading to a stunning viewpoint overlooking the fjord.

Kayaking on Geirangerfjord – Paddle through the serene waters surrounded by some of Norway's most spectacular scenery.

Hidden Gem: Herdalssetra Mountain Farm

A traditional Norwegian farm that has been in operation for over 300 years, where you can taste locally made goat cheese and see how rural life has remained unchanged for centuries.

Flåm – A Scenic Railway Paradise

Flåm is a charming village located deep in the Aurlandsfjord and is famous for being home to one of the world's most scenic rail journeys—the **Flåm Railway**.

Top Attractions & Activities

Flåm Railway (Flåmsbana) – This legendary train ride takes you on a spectacular journey through deep valleys, cascading waterfalls, and snow-capped mountains.

Nærøyfjord Cruise – A boat trip through this UNESCO-listed fjord, one of the narrowest and most beautiful in Norway.

Stegastein Viewpoint – A dramatic lookout point perched 650 meters above the Aurlandsfjord, offering breathtaking views.

Viking Valley Gudvangen – Step back in time and experience a reconstructed Viking village with interactive exhibits, storytelling, and traditional crafts.

Hidden Gem: Brekkefossen Waterfall Hike

A short but rewarding hike offering an incredible view of the waterfall and Flåm valley.

Ålesund – The Art Nouveau City

Ålesund is one of Norway's most unique cities, known for its stunning **Art Nouveau architecture** and breathtaking coastal views. The city was rebuilt in this distinctive style after a devastating fire in 1904, creating a picturesque urban landscape unlike anywhere else in Norway.

Top Attractions & Activities

Aksla Viewpoint – Climb the 418 steps to the top of **Mount Aksla** for an unforgettable view of Ålesund's colorful buildings and surrounding islands.

Atlanterhavsparken (Atlantic Sea Park) – One of the largest saltwater aquariums in Northern Europe, featuring native marine life such as cod, halibut, and even playful seals.

Sunnmøre Museum – An open-air museum showcasing traditional Norwegian wooden boats and Viking artifacts.

Runde Bird Island – A paradise for birdwatchers, home to one of Norway's largest puffin colonies.

Hidden Gem: Alnes Lighthouse

A scenic coastal lighthouse on **Godøy Island**, offering panoramic ocean views and a cozy café serving homemade Norwegian waffles.

Tromsø – The Arctic Capital

If your cruise takes you above the Arctic Circle, you'll likely stop in **Tromsø**, a city known for its **Northern Lights, Midnight Sun, and Arctic adventures**.

Top Attractions & Activities

Arctic Cathedral – An architectural masterpiece resembling ice shards, beautifully illuminated at night.

Fjellheisen Cable Car – Ride to the top of **Storsteinen Mountain** for incredible views of Tromsø and the surrounding fjords.

Northern Lights Tours – Tromsø is one of the best places in the world to see the **Aurora Borealis** during the winter months.

Dog Sledding & Sami Culture – Experience the Arctic wilderness with a thrilling dog sled ride, and learn about Norway's indigenous **Sami people** and their reindeer herding traditions.

Hidden Gem: Polaria Museum

A unique Arctic experience center where you can watch bearded seals swim in an indoor habitat and learn about polar research.

Honningsvåg – Gateway to the North Cape

Honningsvåg is the last major settlement before reaching **Nordkapp (North Cape)**, the northernmost point of mainland Europe.

Top Attractions & Activities

North Cape (Nordkapp) – Stand at the edge of a 307-meter-high cliff overlooking the Arctic Ocean, where the Midnight Sun shines 24 hours a day in summer.

King Crab Safari – Join a local fisherman to catch and feast on **Norwegian King Crab**, a delicacy of the Arctic.

Hurtigruten Coastal Express Museum – Learn about the legendary coastal voyages that have connected Norway's remote communities for over a century.

Hidden Gem: Gjesværstappan Bird Sanctuary

A remote island teeming with seabirds, including puffins, gannets, and sea eagles.

NORWEGIAN FJORDS – THE HEART OF THE CRUISE

Norway's fjords are the true stars of any cruise through this breathtaking Scandinavian country. These deep, glacially carved waterways are among the most dramatic landscapes on Earth, where sheer cliffs rise thousands of feet above emerald-green waters, and waterfalls tumble down from snow-capped peaks. Cruising through the fjords offers an unparalleled perspective, allowing you to glide between towering rock formations, spot wildlife, and visit remote villages that are often inaccessible by land.

This chapter will take you through the magic of Norway's fjords, exploring what makes them so special, the best ways to experience them, and the top fjords you must visit on your cruise.

What Makes Norway's Fjords So Special?

The fjords of Norway were formed during the Ice Age, when massive glaciers carved deep valleys into the landscape. As the glaciers retreated, seawater flooded these valleys, creating the fjords we see today. This unique geological process has resulted in some of the most breathtaking scenery on the planet, with steep cliffs, lush greenery, and pristine waters.

Beyond their beauty, Norway's fjords are rich in history and culture. For centuries, they have been home to Viking settlements, fishing communities, and remote farms that cling to the mountainsides. Today, they are one of the most visited natural wonders in the world, attracting travelers who want to experience Norway's raw, untouched beauty.

The Most Spectacular Fjords to Visit

While Norway is home to over **1,000 fjords**, some stand out as must-visit destinations on any cruise. These fjords are the most breathtaking, historically significant, and accessible via major cruise routes.

Geirangerfjord – Norway's Most Iconic Fjord
Why Visit?

Geirangerfjord is often called the "Jewel of the Fjords," and for good reason. This UNESCO-listed fjord is one of the most photographed in Norway, with dramatic cliffs, thundering waterfalls, and tiny mountain farms perched high above the water.

Top Highlights:

Seven Sisters Waterfall: A breathtaking cascade of seven separate streams plunging from the cliffs into the fjord below.

The Suitor Waterfall: Located directly across from the Seven Sisters, this waterfall is said to be "courting" the sisters.

Eagle Road: A series of 11 hairpin bends offering panoramic views of the fjord.

Dalsnibba Skywalk: One of the highest fjord viewpoints in Europe, providing jaw-dropping vistas of Geirangerfjord.

Sognefjord – The King of the Fjords

Why Visit?

At **204 kilometers (127 miles) long** and **1,308 meters (4,291 feet) deep**, Sognefjord is Norway's longest and deepest fjord. Often called the "King of the Fjords," it stretches from the Atlantic coast into the heart of Norway, with countless smaller branches offering some of the most spectacular scenery in the country.

Top Highlights:

Nærøyfjord: A UNESCO-listed branch of Sognefjord, this narrow fjord is surrounded by towering cliffs and is often considered the most beautiful in Norway.

Flåm Railway: One of the world's most scenic train rides, climbing from fjord level to the mountains, passing waterfalls and dramatic landscapes.

Urnes Stave Church: One of Norway's oldest and most beautifully preserved stave churches, dating back to the 12th century.

Hardangerfjord – The Orchard of Norway

Why Visit?

Known for its picturesque fruit orchards and stunning waterfalls, Hardangerfjord is a gentler yet equally stunning alternative to some of the more dramatic fjords. In spring, the hillsides are covered in blooming apple, cherry, and pear trees, creating a breathtaking contrast against the deep blue waters.

Top Highlights:

Trolltunga Hike: One of Norway's most famous hikes, leading to a spectacular rock formation jutting out 700 meters above the fjord.

Vøringsfossen Waterfall: One of Norway's most powerful waterfalls, dropping 182 meters into the canyon below.

Fruit Orchards: Visit during the harvest season to taste fresh Norwegian apples and cider.

Nærøyfjord – The Narrow Wonder

Why Visit?
This fjord, a branch of Sognefjord, is one of the narrowest in Norway, with sheer cliffs rising more than a thousand meters on either side. A cruise through Nærøyfjord feels like gliding through a fantasy landscape, with waterfalls and tiny villages dotting the shoreline.

Top Highlights:

Kayaking on Nærøyfjord: Get up close to the towering cliffs and hidden waterfalls.

Gudvangen Viking Village: Experience Viking life in a reconstructed village with interactive exhibits.

Winter Cruises: In the colder months, the fjord takes on a magical, frozen beauty, with snow-covered peaks and icy waters.

Lysefjord – Home of Pulpit Rock

Why Visit?
This fjord in southwestern Norway is famous for its dramatic rock formations, including **Preikestolen (Pulpit Rock)**, one of the most photographed cliffs in the world.

Top Highlights:

Hike to Pulpit Rock: A challenging but rewarding hike leading to a flat rock platform with a sheer drop of 604 meters.

Kjeragbolten: A massive boulder wedged between two cliffs, accessible via a tough but exhilarating hike.

Lysefjord Boat Tours: Take a scenic cruise to admire the fjord's rugged beauty from the water.

Wildlife & Nature in the Fjords

Norway's fjords are not just about stunning landscapes—they are also home to diverse wildlife. Keep an eye out for:

Whales: Humpback, minke, and orca whales can often be spotted in the fjords.

Puffins: These charming seabirds' nest along the cliffs during the summer months.

Sea Eagles: The fjords are home to Europe's largest population of white-tailed sea eagles.

Seals & Otters: These playful marine animals can sometimes be seen lounging on the rocky shores.

Best Ways to Experience the Fjords

Cruise Ship Deck Views

One of the best things about a Norwegian fjord cruise is that you don't even need to leave the ship to enjoy the scenery. Make sure to spend time on deck with your camera ready as you glide through these natural wonders.

Kayaking & Small Boat Tours

For a more immersive experience, consider joining a kayaking excursion or a small boat tour. Paddling through the still waters of the fjords allows you to appreciate their grandeur from a unique perspective.

Hiking & Scenic Overlooks

Many fjords have incredible hiking trails leading to viewpoints that offer breathtaking vistas. **Pulpit Rock, Trolltunga, and Dalsnibba** are some of the most famous.

Scenic Train Rides

The **Flåm Railway** and **Rauma Railway** offer some of the most stunning rail journeys in the world, providing a different perspective on the fjords from above.

SHORE EXCURSIONS & ACTIVITIES

A Norwegian cruise is not just about breathtaking scenery from the deck—it's about stepping off the ship and immersing yourself in the natural wonders, history, and culture of Norway. Shore excursions allow you to experience the fjords, mountains, and charming villages up close, offering everything from scenic hikes and thrilling boat rides to cultural tours and wildlife encounters.

This chapter will explore the best shore excursions available in Norway, categorized by activity type. Whether you're an adrenaline seeker, history buff, or nature lover, there's something for everyone to enjoy during your cruise stops.

Must-Try Fjord Boat Tours & Kayaking Adventures

Fjord Cruises: The Best Way to See the Scenery

While your main cruise ship provides stunning views, nothing compares to sailing through the fjords on a smaller boat. These excursions allow you to get closer to waterfalls, explore hidden inlets, and experience the serenity of Norway's famous waterways.

Best Fjord Boat Tours

Geirangerfjord RIB Boat Tour: A thrilling ride on a **rigid inflatable boat (RIB)** that takes you close to the **Seven Sisters Waterfall** and abandoned fjord farms perched on cliffs.

Nærøyfjord UNESCO Heritage Cruise: A leisurely journey through one of the world's narrowest fjords, surrounded by towering cliffs and charming villages.

Lysefjord & Pulpit Rock Cruise: A scenic boat tour beneath the famous **Preikestolen (Pulpit Rock)**, with stops at caves and remote waterfalls.

Kayaking: A Peaceful and Immersive Experience

Kayaking in the fjords offers an intimate way to explore Norway's waterways, allowing you to paddle through still waters while taking in the stunning scenery around you.

Best Kayaking Locations

Flåm & Aurlandsfjord: Paddle along calm waters with views of snow-capped mountains and tiny villages.

Geirangerfjord: Kayak under towering cliffs and beside cascading waterfalls.

Tromsø: In Arctic Norway, kayak through crystal-clear waters while spotting wildlife like seals and seabirds.

Tip: Kayaking excursions are often available for both beginners and experienced paddlers, with guides providing safety instructions and gear.

Scenic Railway Journeys

Norway is home to some of the world's most breathtaking train rides. A scenic railway excursion allows you to experience the fjords and mountains from a completely different perspective, traveling through lush valleys, steep gorges, and snowy peaks.

The Best Train Excursions

Flåm Railway – A Must-Do Excursion

What Makes It Special? Known as one of the most scenic train journeys in the world, the **Flåm Railway** takes you from the fjord village of Flåm up to the high mountain station of Myrdal, passing waterfalls, deep valleys, and lush forests.

Excursion Tip: Combine it with a boat tour on Nærøyfjord for a full-day fjord experience.

Rauma Railway – A Hidden Gem

What Makes It Special? This lesser-known railway travels through some of Norway's most stunning landscapes, passing the famous **Trollveggen (Troll Wall)**, the tallest vertical rock face in Europe.

Excursion Tip: If your cruise stops in Åndalsnes, this is one of the best excursions to book.

Bergen Railway – A Journey Across Norway

What Makes It Special? Connecting Oslo to Bergen, this scenic train journey crosses the **Hardangervidda Plateau**, one of Europe's largest mountain plateaus.

Hiking Norway's Most Famous Trails

If you love hiking, Norway offers some of the most spectacular trails in the world. Many cruise ports provide access to trails that lead to breathtaking viewpoints.

Top Hiking Excursions

Pulpit Rock (Preikestolen) – Stavanger

Why Go? One of Norway's most famous hikes, leading to a flat rock platform towering 604 meters above Lysefjord.

Difficulty: Moderate (8 km round-trip, 4–5 hours).

Excursion Tip: Wear sturdy hiking boots and bring water.

Trolltunga – Hardangerfjord

Why Go? This challenging hike leads to an epic rock formation jutting out over the fjord, creating one of Norway's most iconic views.

Difficulty: Very difficult (20 km round-trip, 10–12 hours).

Excursion Tip: Only for experienced hikers—consider an overnight stay.

Romsdalseggen Ridge – Åndalsnes

Why Go? One of Norway's most scenic hikes, offering panoramic views of fjords, mountains, and waterfalls.

Difficulty: Strenuous (10 km, 6–7 hours).

Mount Fløyen – Bergen

Why Go? A relatively easy hike with stunning views over Bergen and the surrounding islands.

Difficulty: Easy to moderate (5 km round-trip, 1–2 hours).

Sami Culture & Reindeer Encounters in the Arctic

If your cruise takes you above the Arctic Circle, don't miss the chance to experience **Sami culture**, the indigenous people of Norway's north.

Best Excursions for Sami Culture

Reindeer Sledding (Tromsø & Alta): Ride through snowy landscapes with a Sami guide while learning about traditional reindeer herding.

Sami Lavvu Experience: Visit a traditional Sami tent (lavvu), enjoy a meal cooked over an open fire, and listen to Sami joik (a type of singing).

Northern Lights Sami Experience: In winter, join a Sami guide for an aurora-watching tour while learning about their folklore and traditions.

Wildlife Safaris & Whale Watching

Norway's fjords and Arctic waters are home to incredible wildlife. A guided wildlife safari is one of the best ways to experience Norway's diverse ecosystems.

Best Wildlife Excursions

Whale Watching in Tromsø & Andenes: See orcas, humpbacks, and sperm whales in their natural habitat.

Puffin Safari in Runde: Visit one of Norway's largest puffin colonies.

Sea Eagle Safari in Lofoten: Spot Europe's largest bird of prey as it soars above the fjords.

Arctic Circle Adventures: Dog Sledding & Snowmobiling

For those cruising to Northern Norway in winter, **dog sledding and snowmobiling** offer thrilling ways to experience the Arctic landscape.

Best Excursions for Arctic Adventures

Dog Sledding in Tromsø & Alta: A high-energy ride through snowy forests and tundra, led by a team of enthusiastic huskies.

Snowmobiling in Kirkenes: Explore frozen fjords and mountain plateaus at high speed.

Ice Fishing & King Crab Safari: Try your hand at ice fishing and enjoy a fresh seafood meal in a traditional Sami tent.

ONBOARD CRUISE EXPERIENCE

A Norwegian cruise is not just about the breathtaking destinations—it's also about the experience onboard. Your ship is your floating home, offering luxurious comforts, fine dining, and endless entertainment as you sail through fjords, past glaciers, and beneath the Northern Lights. Whether you're enjoying a spa treatment with panoramic views, savoring fresh seafood in a fine-dining restaurant, or attending an enrichment lecture on Viking history, your cruise ship enhances the overall journey in countless ways.

In this chapter, we'll explore everything you need to know about the **onboard experience**, from dining and entertainment to wellness facilities and Northern Lights viewing.

What to Expect on a Norway Cruise Ship

Each cruise line offers a different experience, from large resort-style ships packed with activities to small, expedition-style vessels designed for in-depth exploration. No matter which ship you choose, expect stunning views from every deck, as the Norwegian coastline is one of the most scenic in the world.

Types of Ships & Onboard Atmosphere

Large Cruise Ships (1,500+ passengers)

Luxurious, with multiple restaurants, theaters, casinos, and pools.

Family-friendly with kids' clubs and entertainment.

Examples: Royal Caribbean, MSC, Norwegian Cruise Line.

Mid-Sized & Premium Cruise Ships (500–1,500 passengers)

More intimate and refined, with upscale dining and personalized service.

Offers a good balance between adventure and comfort.

Examples: Viking Cruises, Holland America Line, Celebrity Cruises.

Small & Expedition Ships (50–500 passengers)

Focuses on nature, adventure, and cultural experiences.

Fewer amenities but offers unique excursions, such as Zodiac landings in remote areas.

Examples: Hurtigruten, Ponant, Silversea Expeditions.

Regardless of ship size, **Norwegian cruises tend to have a relaxed atmosphere**, with most guests dressing comfortably. Formal nights, if they exist, are usually optional.

Dining & Norwegian Cuisine Onboard

Dining on a Norway cruise is an experience in itself, with many ships incorporating **local Norwegian flavors** into their menus. Whether you're indulging in fresh seafood, enjoying a gourmet steak, or sipping coffee while gazing at glaciers, meals onboard are designed to be as memorable as the destinations.

Main Dining Options

Buffet Restaurants: Most cruise lines offer a buffet featuring international cuisine alongside Norwegian specialties like smoked salmon and reindeer stew.

Main Dining Rooms: These provide multi-course meals in a more formal setting, with dishes inspired by Scandinavian and global flavors.

Specialty Restaurants: Many ships have exclusive dining venues offering **fine steaks, seafood, Italian, French, or Asian cuisine**. Some premium lines include **Nordic fine-dining experiences**.

Norwegian Dishes to Try Onboard

Gravlax (Cured Salmon): Often served with mustard sauce and rye bread.

Klippfisk (Dried & Salted Cod): A classic dish from the Norwegian coast.

Kjøttkaker (Norwegian Meatballs): Served with potatoes and brown sauce.

Brunost (Brown Cheese): A caramelized cheese with a sweet, nutty flavor.

Skrei (Winter Cod): A delicacy available during the colder months.

Beverage Selections

Norwegian cruises offer a **wide range of drinks**, from fine wines to locally brewed craft beer. **Akvavit**, a traditional Norwegian spirit, is a must-try for those interested in local flavors. Some cruise lines also serve hot drinks on deck during cold-weather sailings, such as **gløgg (spiced mulled wine)** and **hot chocolate with cloudberries**.

Entertainment & Enrichment Programs

While the Norwegian landscape provides plenty of entertainment on its own, cruise ships offer a variety of activities and performances to enhance your journey.

Live Performances & Shows

Theater Productions: Larger ships often feature Broadway-style musicals, comedy shows, or concerts.

Live Music: Many cruise lines have **Norwegian folk music performances** or jazz evenings in onboard lounges.

Cultural Shows: Some cruises feature storytelling about **Viking legends** or performances showcasing **Sami traditions**.

Enrichment Lectures & Workshops

To deepen your understanding of Norway's history and culture, many ships offer **educational talks and hands-on workshops**:

Viking History Lectures: Learn about Norway's seafaring ancestors and visit Viking-themed exhibitions.

Photography Workshops: Perfect for capturing fjords, Northern Lights, and Arctic landscapes.

Wildlife Talks: Marine biologists often host sessions about **whales, puffins, and Arctic foxes**.

Expedition Cruises: On **Hurtigruten and similar adventure ships**, enrichment programs are even more immersive, with onboard experts leading guided hikes, nature walks, and Zodiac tours.

Wellness & Relaxation: Spas, Pools & Outdoor Hot Tubs

After a day of exploring, nothing beats unwinding at the spa, soaking in a hot tub, or enjoying a sauna session with stunning fjord views.

Onboard Spa & Wellness Facilities

Thermal Suites & Saunas: Many ships offer Scandinavian-inspired wellness centers with **steam rooms, saunas, and heated loungers** overlooking the ocean.

Outdoor Hot Tubs & Infinity Pools: Some premium cruises, like Viking Ocean Cruises, feature infinity pools that make you feel as though you're floating on the fjords.

Massage & Beauty Treatments: Indulge in Norwegian-inspired treatments, such as **Arctic seaweed wraps** or **glacial stone massages**.

Tip: On cold-weather cruises, relaxing in an outdoor hot tub while watching the fjords pass by is one of the most magical experiences.

Northern Lights Viewing & Midnight Sun Experiences

Norwegian cruises offer some of the most **spectacular natural light shows on Earth**—the **Northern Lights in winter** and the **Midnight Sun in summer**.

Chasing the Northern Lights

If you're cruising **between September and March**, your ship may travel above the Arctic Circle to maximize your chances of witnessing the **Aurora Borealis**.

Best Viewing Locations:

Tromsø

Alta

Honningsvåg (North Cape)

Onboard Announcements: Many ships have an **Aurora alert system** so you won't miss a sighting.

Photography Tips: Use a tripod and set your camera to long exposure for the best shots.

The Magic of the Midnight Sun

If you're sailing in **June or July**, the **Midnight Sun** provides **24 hours of daylight**, creating surreal landscapes where the sun never sets.

Best Places to Experience It:

Lofoten Islands

Svalbard

North Cape

Tip: Many ships host **special Midnight Sun deck parties**, complete with music, drinks, and storytelling.

Shopping & Souvenirs Onboard

Most Norwegian cruise ships have onboard shops offering duty-free goods and unique souvenirs.

What to Buy?

Norwegian Wool Sweaters: Made from high-quality wool and featuring traditional Nordic patterns.

Reindeer Leather & Sami Handicrafts: Beautiful handmade souvenirs from Arctic Norway.

Cloudberry Jam: A rare Nordic delicacy made from wild Arctic berries.

Akvavit & Norwegian Spirits: Traditional Scandinavian liquors.

NORWAY'S RICH CULTURE & TRADITIONS

Norway is more than just dramatic fjords and breathtaking landscapes—it is a country with a deep-rooted culture that reflects its Viking heritage, folklore, and unique traditions. Whether you're exploring the bustling cities of Bergen and Oslo or visiting remote Arctic villages, you'll find that Norway's customs, celebrations, and way of life are closely connected to its natural surroundings.

In this chapter, we'll explore the **rich cultural heritage of Norway**, from its legendary Viking past to the unique traditions of the indigenous Sami people. We'll also dive into **Norwegian festivals, folklore, food culture, and the Scandinavian way of life**, helping you gain a deeper appreciation for this extraordinary country.

Viking Heritage & History

No discussion of Norwegian culture is complete without mentioning the **Vikings**, the legendary seafarers who dominated Scandinavia from the **8th to the 11th century**. Norway's fjords and coastline were home to some of the most powerful Viking chieftains, and remnants of this era can still be seen today.

Who Were the Vikings?

The Vikings were not just fierce warriors—they were also explorers, traders, and skilled shipbuilders. Norwegian Vikings sailed to **Greenland, Iceland, and even North America** (500 years before Columbus). Their advanced shipbuilding techniques allowed them to cross vast oceans, and their society was surprisingly complex, with a system of laws, craftsmanship, and trade.

Best Places to Explore Viking History

Viking Ship Museum (Oslo): Home to some of the world's best-preserved Viking ships, including the famous Oseberg ship.

Lofotr Viking Museum (Lofoten Islands): A reconstructed Viking chieftain's longhouse where you can experience Viking feasts, archery, and storytelling.

Avaldsnes (Near Haugesund): An ancient Viking settlement where Norway's first kings ruled.

Did You Know? The word "Viking" comes from the Old Norse word "víkingr," meaning "pirate" or "raider." However, most Vikings were not raiders—they were farmers and traders.

Norwegian Festivals & Celebrations

Norwegians love their festivals, and many of their **traditional celebrations** are tied to their Viking roots, Christian heritage, and seasonal changes.

National Day – May 17th (Syttende Mai)

Norway's Constitution Day is the **biggest national celebration of the year**, with parades, traditional clothing, and plenty of food. People dress in **bunads** (traditional Norwegian outfits) and wave flags as they march through the streets.

Midsummer's Eve (St. Hans Aften) – June 23rd

Celebrated with **bonfires, music, and dancing**, this festival marks the **summer solstice**, the longest day of the year. In northern Norway, where the sun never sets in summer, the celebrations are even more magical.

Northern Lights Festival (Tromsø) – January

A winter festival dedicated to **music and art**, held during the **Northern Lights season** in Arctic Norway.

Sami National Day (February 6th)

A celebration of Norway's indigenous **Sami people**, featuring **reindeer races, joik singing, and cultural performances**.

Tip: If you're cruising in summer, try to catch a local festival—it's the best way to experience Norwegian culture firsthand.

Sami Indigenous Culture & Arctic Traditions

The **Sami people** are the indigenous inhabitants of northern Norway, Sweden, Finland, and parts of Russia. They have lived in Arctic Scandinavia for thousands of years, developing a **nomadic lifestyle centered around reindeer herding**.

Who Is the Sami?

The Sami were traditionally **reindeer herders, fishermen, and hunters**, adapting to the harsh Arctic environment.

They have their own **language, flag, and national day (February 6th).**

Their traditional homes, called **lavvus**, resemble Native American tipis and were designed for easy movement with reindeer herds.

Best Ways to Experience Sami Culture

Tromsø & Alta: Visit a Sami reindeer farm and learn about their traditions.

Karasjok & Kautokeino: The heart of Sami culture in Norway, featuring museums and festivals.

Sami Parliament (Karasjok): Norway has a **separate parliament for the Sami people**, reflecting their unique status.

Joik – The Sami Form of Singing

One of the most **distinctive aspects of Sami culture** is **joik**, a haunting, melodic singing style that is often used to **tell stories or honor nature and ancestors**. It is one of Europe's oldest musical traditions.

Did You Know? The Disney movie *Frozen* was inspired by Sami culture, and its music incorporates elements of **joik**!

Norwegian Folklore & Mythology

Norway is filled with **mystical tales of trolls, elves, and hidden creatures**, many of which originated in the Viking Age and have been passed down for generations.

Trolls: Norway's Most Famous Mythical Creatures

According to legend, **trolls live in the mountains and forests** of Norway. They are usually giant, slow-witted, and turn to stone when exposed to sunlight. Many of Norway's rock formations are said to be **trolls that were caught in the sun and frozen forever**.

Famous Folklore Sites

Trollstigen (Troll's Path): A winding mountain road with dramatic scenery, named after the trolls.

Trolltunga (Troll's Tongue): A famous rock formation that resembles a troll's tongue sticking out.

Other Mythical Creatures in Norwegian Folklore

Nøkken: A water spirit that lures people into lakes.

Huldra: A beautiful forest maiden with a hidden cow's tail.

Draugr: Undead Viking warriors who haunt grave mounds.

Tip: If you visit **Norwegian gift shops**, you'll find troll figurines everywhere—these make great souvenirs!

The Scandinavian Lifestyle: "Kos" & Outdoor Living

Norwegians embrace a simple, cozy lifestyle known as **"kos"**, which is similar to the Danish concept of **"hygge"**. It's all about **enjoying life's little pleasures**, whether it's a cup of hot chocolate by the fireplace or a long hike in the mountains.

Friluftsliv – The Love of Nature

Friluftsliv (literally "open-air life") is the Norwegian philosophy of spending time outdoors, regardless of the weather.

Many Norwegians **go hiking, skiing, or fishing year-round**, even in deep winter.

There is a strong **"right to roam" (Allemannsretten)** law, meaning that everyone has the right to access nature, even private land.

Kos – The Art of Coziness

Candlelit evenings with friends and family.

Slow-cooked meals and warm drinks.

Enjoying the simple moments, whether alone or with loved ones.

Tip: If you're on a winter cruise, embrace **"kos"** by bundling up with a blanket, sipping hot gløgg, and watching the Northern Lights from the deck!

PRACTICAL TRAVEL TIPS & ESSENTIALS

Traveling through Norway on a cruise is an unforgettable experience, but to make the most of your journey, it's important to be well-prepared. From understanding Norwegian currency and language to knowing how to handle unpredictable weather, a little preparation goes a long way.

This chapter will guide you through the **essential travel tips** for navigating Norway smoothly, ensuring that your trip is enjoyable, stress-free, and filled with amazing experiences.

Norwegian Currency, Costs & Payment Methods

Norwegian Krone (NOK) – The Local Currency

Norway does not use the Euro. Instead, its official currency is the **Norwegian Krone (NOK)**. One krone is divided into 100 øre, though øre coins are no longer in circulation.

Exchange Rate: 1 USD ≈ 10 NOK (varies).

Common Bills: 50 NOK, 100 NOK, 200 NOK, 500 NOK, and 1,000 NOK.

Common Coins: 1 NOK, 5 NOK, 10 NOK, 20 NOK.

Is Norway Expensive? Understanding Costs

Norway is known for being one of the most expensive countries in the world, and cruise travelers should budget accordingly.

Dining Out: A meal at a mid-range restaurant can cost **200–400 NOK per person**.

Coffee: A simple black coffee can cost **40–60 NOK** in a café.

Beer or Wine: A pint of beer in a pub costs around **90–120 NOK**.

Public Transport: A single bus ticket in major cities costs **40–50 NOK**.

Souvenirs: A Norwegian wool sweater costs around **1,500 NOK**, while small souvenirs like troll figurines start at **100 NOK**.

Best Ways to Pay in Norway

Norway is almost a **cashless society**, and credit or debit cards are widely accepted.

Visa & Mastercard are the most commonly accepted cards.

American Express is accepted in larger cities but not everywhere.

Mobile Payments (VIPPS, Apple Pay, Google Pay) are popular, especially in cafés and stores.

ATMs (Minibank) are available, but most visitors rarely need cash.

Tip: Always check if your bank charges foreign transaction fees before using your card abroad.

Language Tips & Common Norwegian Phrases

Is English Widely Spoken in Norway?

Yes! Most Norwegians speak excellent **English**, especially in cities and tourist areas. However, learning a few Norwegian phrases can enhance your experience and show respect for the local culture.

Essential Norwegian Phrases

English	Norwegian	Pronunciation
Hello	Hei	"Hi"
Good morning	God morgen	"Goo mor-gun"
Thank you	Takk	"Tack"
Yes	Ja	"Yah"
No	Nei	"Nay"
How much does it cost?	Hvor mye koster det?	"Vore mye kost-er deh?"
Excuse me	Unnskyld meg	"Oon-shild my"
Do you speak English?	Snakker du engelsk?	"Snahk-er doo eng-elsk?"
Cheers!	Skål!	"Skol!"

Tip: Norwegians appreciate when visitors try to say **takk (thank you)** after a meal or service.

Internet & Connectivity at Sea

Wi-Fi on Cruise Ships

Most cruise ships offer **Wi-Fi**, but it can be **expensive and slow** due to satellite connections. Some cruise lines offer **free Wi-Fi packages**, but others charge **$10–$30 per day**.

Mobile Network & Roaming in Norway

Norway has **excellent mobile coverage**, even in fjord regions. Major Norwegian networks include:

Telenor

Telia

Ice

If you're from the **EU**, your mobile plan may include **free roaming in Norway**. For travelers from **the U.S., Canada, or Australia**, international roaming can be expensive. Consider:

Buying a Norwegian SIM Card at the airport or a convenience store.

Using an eSIM (digital SIM) for affordable data.

Activating a global roaming plan from your home provider.

Travel Insurance & Health Precautions
Why You Need Travel Insurance

Norway has **excellent healthcare**, but medical treatment for visitors **can be expensive**. A simple doctor's visit could cost **1,000 NOK ($100)**, and emergency medical treatment could be even higher.

A good **travel insurance policy** should cover:

Medical emergencies & hospital visits.

Trip cancellations & delays.

Lost or stolen belongings.

Adventure activities (hiking, kayaking, etc.).

Tip: If your cruise includes Arctic Norway or Svalbard, make sure your insurance covers **emergency**

evacuation—there are no hospitals in remote Arctic areas.

Health Precautions for Norway

No vaccinations are required for entry into Norway.

Tap water is 100% safe to drink and some of the cleanest in the world.

Bring seasickness medication if you're prone to motion sickness, especially when sailing the **North Sea or Arctic waters**.

Sustainable & Responsible Travel in Norway

Norway is one of the most environmentally conscious countries in the world. Visitors are encouraged to **travel responsibly and protect nature**.

How to Be a Responsible Traveler

Respect "Allemannsretten" (Right to Roam): You are allowed to explore Norway's nature freely, but you must leave no trace.

Avoid Plastic Waste: Bring a **reusable water bottle**—Norwegian tap water is pure and delicious.

Use Public Transport: Norway has excellent trains, buses, and ferries that reduce environmental impact.

Choose Eco-Friendly Tours: Many tour companies now offer **electric fjord boats and sustainable wildlife safaris**.

Follow the "Leave No Trace" Rule: Don't litter, don't disturb wildlife, and stay on marked trails when hiking.

Tip: In some fjords, like **Geirangerfjord**, cruise ships must meet strict **zero-emission regulations** to protect the environment.

Safety & Emergency Contacts

Norway is one of the **safest countries in the world**, but it's still important to be aware of potential risks.

Emergency Numbers in Norway

Emergency Service Number

Police   112

Ambulance   113

Emergency Service Number

Fire   110

General Emergency   112

Safety Tips for Norway

Crime is very low, but pickpocketing can occur in busy tourist areas.

Weather can change rapidly, especially in the mountains—always bring extra layers.

Watch out for slippery roads and trails in winter, even in the cities.

Tip: If hiking, always check the **yr.no** weather app, which is Norway's most accurate forecast service.

SPECIAL INTEREST CRUISES & UNIQUE EXPERIENCES

Not all Norwegian cruises are the same. While classic fjord cruises are a fantastic way to explore Norway's coastline, there are also **specialized cruises** designed for those who want something beyond the usual itinerary. Whether you're chasing the **Northern Lights in winter**, experiencing the surreal **Midnight Sun in summer**, embarking on an **expedition cruise to Svalbard**, or joining a **luxury small-ship voyage**, Norway offers extraordinary cruise experiences tailored to different interests.

In this chapter, we'll explore the **most unique Norwegian cruise experiences**, helping you find the perfect voyage that matches your sense of adventure, comfort, and curiosity.

Northern Lights Winter Cruises

What Makes a Northern Lights Cruise Special?

The **Aurora Borealis**, or **Northern Lights**, is one of nature's most incredible spectacles. These dancing green, purple, and red lights illuminate the Arctic sky in winter, creating a magical, otherworldly experience.

While the Northern Lights can be seen from land, a cruise offers the **perfect viewing conditions**, away from city lights, with dark Arctic skies stretching endlessly over the ocean.

Best Time to Take a Northern Lights Cruise

Season: September to March

Peak Months: December to February (longer nights, higher chances of seeing the aurora)

Best Locations: Above the Arctic Circle, in cities like **Tromsø, Alta, Honningsvåg (North Cape), and Kirkenes**

What to Expect on a Northern Lights Cruise

Aurora Alerts: Many cruise lines have **aurora tracking systems** that notify passengers when the Northern Lights appear.

Onboard Astronomy Lectures: Experts explain the science behind the auroras and provide **stargazing insights**.

Outdoor Hot Tubs & Viewing Decks: Imagine watching the Northern Lights while relaxing in a **heated jacuzzi on deck**!

Photography Workshops: Learn how to capture the perfect aurora shot from professional photographers onboard.

Top Cruise Lines for Northern Lights Cruises

Hurtigruten: Specializes in Arctic and expedition cruises with **aurora guarantees** (if you don't see the lights, they offer a free cruise!).

Viking Ocean Cruises: Offers a luxury Northern Lights experience with fine dining and spa amenities.

Ponant & Silversea Expeditions: For a more exclusive, small-ship Arctic adventure.

Midnight Sun Summer Voyages
What Makes a Midnight Sun Cruise Special?

During summer, **above the Arctic Circle**, the sun never sets for weeks at a time. This phenomenon, known as the **Midnight Sun**, creates a surreal golden glow that lasts through the night, allowing for extended outdoor adventures.

Best Time for a Midnight Sun Cruise

Season: Late May to late July

Best Locations: Northern Norway, including **Lofoten Islands, Tromsø, North Cape, and Svalbard**

Unique Midnight Sun Experiences

Hiking at Midnight: Many cruises offer special **late-night hikes under the golden sun**, with breathtaking Arctic landscapes illuminated in warm light.

Kayaking & Wildlife Watching: Midnight boat tours allow you to spot **whales, puffins, and seals** in the glowing summer sky.

Midnight Sun Deck Parties: Enjoy **champagne and live music** as you celebrate daylight at midnight.

Top Cruise Lines for Midnight Sun Cruises

Hurtigruten: Classic Norwegian coastal voyages with an emphasis on nature.

Viking Cruises: Offers luxury small-ship experiences with scenic fjord routes.

Windstar Cruises: A boutique experience with smaller ships for a more intimate journey.

Expedition Cruises to Svalbard & the Arctic
What Makes a Svalbard Cruise Special?

Svalbard, an **archipelago between mainland Norway and the North Pole**, is one of the **world's last great wildernesses**. This frozen paradise is home to **polar bears, glaciers, and untouched Arctic landscapes**.

Unlike regular cruises, **expedition cruises** to Svalbard offer **smaller ships, expert-led excursions, and Zodiac landings** in remote areas.

Best Time to Visit Svalbard

Summer (June–August): Midnight Sun, Arctic wildlife, and glacier hikes.

Winter (March–April): Frozen landscapes, Northern Lights, and polar bear sightings.

Unique Experiences on a Svalbard Cruise

Polar Bear Spotting: Svalbard is home to around **3,000 polar bears**, making it one of the best places in the world to see them in the wild.

Glacier Landings: Expedition cruises use **Zodiacs (small inflatable boats)** to land on remote Arctic beaches for glacier hikes.

Ice Caves & Dog Sledding: Some winter cruises offer **ice cave exploration and dog sledding** in Longyearbyen.

Whale & Walrus Watching: The cold Arctic waters around Svalbard are home to **beluga whales, walruses, and narwhals**.

Top Expedition Cruise Lines for Svalbard

Hurtigruten Expeditions: Offers eco-friendly, science-focused Arctic cruises.

Ponant & Silversea Expeditions: Luxury small-ship exploration with expert guides.

Lindblad-National Geographic: Educational cruises with photographers and naturalists onboard.

Photography Cruises: Capturing the Fjords & Arctic Wonders

What Makes a Photography Cruise Special?

Norway is a dream destination for **landscape photographers**, with its **fjords, waterfalls, Northern Lights, and Arctic wildlife** providing endless photo opportunities.

Best Time for a Photography Cruise

Fjords & Waterfalls: Spring (April–June) when waterfalls are at their strongest.

Northern Lights: Winter (September–March).

Midnight Sun: Summer (June–July).

Wildlife Photography: Summer (May–August) for puffins, whales, and Arctic foxes.

Photography Highlights on a Norway Cruise

Dramatic Fjords: Capture the **mirror-like reflections of Geirangerfjord** and **Nærøyfjord**.

Wildlife Action: Photograph **whales breaching in the Arctic waters** or **puffins nesting on cliffs**.

Aurora Borealis: Learn night photography techniques from onboard experts.

Top Cruise Lines for Photography Cruises

Lindblad-National Geographic Expeditions: Features professional photographers on board.

Aurora Expeditions: Specializes in Arctic and fjord photography tours.

Ponant: Small luxury cruises with private photography workshops.

Luxury & Small Ship Cruises vs. Large Cruise Lines

Large Cruise Ships

Pros: More amenities, larger entertainment options, multiple dining choices.

Cons: Can't access smaller fjords, less intimate experience.

Best For: First-time cruisers, families, travelers who enjoy onboard entertainment.

Examples: Royal Caribbean, Norwegian Cruise Line, MSC Cruises.

Small & Luxury Ships

Pros: Can enter narrow fjords, better service, exclusive excursions.

Cons: Higher cost, fewer onboard entertainment options.

Best For: Adventure seekers, photographers, nature lovers, luxury travelers.

Examples: Viking Ocean Cruises, Ponant, Silversea Expeditions, Windstar.

NORWAY CRUISE FAQS & TROUBLESHOOTING

No matter how well you prepare for your Norwegian cruise, you're bound to have questions along the way. From **what to do in case of bad weather** to **how to handle seasickness**, this chapter will answer the most frequently asked questions and provide troubleshooting tips to ensure a **smooth and stress-free cruise experience**.

Whether it's your first time cruising or you're a seasoned traveler, these insights will help you navigate unexpected situations and make the most of your journey through Norway's breathtaking fjords, charming coastal towns, and Arctic landscapes.

What If the Weather Changes?

Understanding Norway's Unpredictable Weather

Norwegian weather is famous for its rapid and unexpected changes. It's possible to experience **sunshine, rain, wind, and even snow** all within a single day—especially in the fjords and Arctic regions.

Summer (June–August): Temperatures range from **10–25°C (50–77°F)** but expect occasional rain showers.

Spring & Autumn (April–May, September–October): Cooler, with temperatures between **5–15°C (41–59°F)** and more unpredictable weather.

Winter (November–March): Cold and snowy, with temperatures between **-10 to 5°C (14–41°F)**, especially in Arctic Norway.

What Happens If an Excursion Is Canceled Due to Weather?

Cruise lines will try to offer an alternative activity (e.g., if a hiking tour is canceled due to rain, you may get a guided city tour instead).

If an excursion is **fully canceled**, you'll receive a **refund or onboard credit**.

Some independent tour operators offer **"weather guarantees,"** allowing you to rebook for another time.

How to Prepare for Sudden Weather Changes

Always pack **layers**, including a **waterproof jacket** and **warm fleece**.

Bring a **compact umbrella** and waterproof shoes.

Carry **a dry bag** to protect electronics like your phone or camera.

Tip: Check the **yr.no** weather app—it's Norway's most accurate forecast service.

How to Handle Seasickness in Norwegian Waters?

Is Seasickness a Concern in Norway?

For the most part, **cruising in Norway is smooth**, especially in the sheltered fjords where waters are calm. However, the **North Sea, Arctic Ocean, and Norwegian Sea** can be rough, particularly in winter.

How to Prevent Seasickness

Choose a Mid-Ship Cabin: Lower decks and mid-ship locations experience less movement.

Take Motion Sickness Medication: Dramamine, Bonine, or **scopolamine patches** work well.

Use Natural Remedies: Ginger tea, peppermint oil, and acupressure wristbands can help.

Stay on Deck & Get Fresh Air: Watching the horizon stabilizes your balance.

Eat Small Meals & Stay Hydrated: Avoid greasy or heavy foods.

Tip: If you're prone to seasickness, choose a cruise that **focuses on fjord routes** rather than open-sea crossings.

What Should I Do If I Miss the Ship?

How Can You Miss a Cruise Ship?

Returning Late from a Shore Excursion: Independent tours that run over time may cause you to miss boarding.

Getting Lost in Port: Large cities like Bergen and Oslo have busy harbors with multiple docks.

Underestimating Walking Time: Some ports require long walks back to the ship.

What to Do If the Ship Leaves Without You

Stay Calm & Contact the Cruise Line Immediately – They may assist in arranging transport to the next port.

Have Your Passport & Travel Insurance Handy – These are essential if you need to book a last-minute flight or ferry.

Find the Nearest Embassy or Consulate (If in a foreign country).

Always Carry Emergency Cash & a Credit Card for unexpected expenses.

How to Avoid Missing the Ship

Always **return to the ship at least 1 hour before departure**.

If booking an **independent tour**, ensure it **guarantees return on time**.

Carry a **port map** and the ship's **emergency contact number**.

Tip: If unsure about independent tours, book **ship-sponsored excursions**, as the cruise **won't leave without you**.

What Should I Do If My Luggage Is Lost?

Lost Luggage at the Airport

If your luggage doesn't arrive, immediately **file a lost baggage claim** with the airline.

Most airlines will **deliver lost bags to your cruise ship** within **24–48 hours**.

Carry a **change of clothes and essentials** in your carry-on.

Lost Luggage at Sea

Report lost items to the ship's **Guest Services desk**.

If lost during an excursion, check with **local authorities or tour operators**.

Keep **valuables (passport, medication, electronics) in your carry-on** rather than checked luggage.

What Happens If I Get Sick on the Cruise?

Medical Facilities on Board

All cruise ships have **medical centers with doctors and nurses** available 24/7. However, these are designed for **basic medical care** rather than major emergencies.

What Medical Costs to Expect

Consultation Fees: $100–$200 per visit.

Medications: Ships have a **small pharmacy**, but expect high prices.

Serious Emergencies: If you need hospital care, you may be **evacuated to the nearest city**.

How to Avoid Medical Issues on a Cruise

Pack Essential Medications (enough for your entire trip + extra).

Stay Hydrated & Eat Carefully (seafood allergies and rich foods can trigger reactions).

Wash Hands Frequently (to prevent Norovirus, a common cruise illness).

Tip: Travel insurance is highly recommended to cover medical emergencies.

How Can I Stay Connected With Family While Cruising?

Internet Options

Most cruise ships offer **Wi-Fi**, but it can be **expensive and slow** (around $10–$30 per day).

Some ports offer **free public Wi-Fi**, especially in cafés and libraries.

Using Your Phone in Norway

EU Travelers: Most European SIM cards work in Norway with no extra charges.

U.S. & Non-EU Travelers: Consider buying a **Norwegian SIM card** for data.

Wi-Fi Calling & Apps: Use WhatsApp, Skype, or Zoom for free communication.

Tip: Some cruise lines now offer **Starlink Internet**, which is much faster than traditional satellite Wi-Fi.

Cruise Etiquette & Local Cultural Norms

Onboard Cruise Etiquette

Respect Quiet Hours: Especially on small luxury ships.

Be Punctual for Excursions & Meals: Arriving late disrupts schedules.

Mind Dress Codes: Some specialty restaurants require **smart casual attire.**

Be Considerate on Deck: Avoid **saving deck chairs for hours**.

Norwegian Cultural Etiquette

Norwegians Value Personal Space: Avoid standing too close when talking.

Tipping is Not Expected: Service charges are already included.

Respect Nature: Littering or damaging the environment is **strongly frowned upon.**

Tip: Norwegians are reserved but friendly—don't be offended if they're not overly chatty!

RESOURCES & FINAL THOUGHTS

As your journey through this **Norwegian cruise guide** comes to an end, it's time to gather all the **essential resources** that will help you plan and execute your trip smoothly. Whether you're still in the **planning phase**, looking for **last-minute packing tips**, or searching for **useful travel apps**, this chapter will serve as your go-to reference.

A Norwegian cruise is a once-in-a-lifetime experience, and by having the **right resources, travel tools, and expert insights**, you'll be well-prepared to enjoy the breathtaking fjords, Arctic landscapes, and rich Nordic culture without stress.

Recommended Books & Travel Guides

While this guide covers nearly everything you need to know, there are some **additional books** that can enrich your knowledge about Norway's history, landscapes, and cultural traditions.

Travel Guidebooks

Rick Steves Scandinavia – A detailed travel guide covering Norway along with Sweden and Denmark, perfect for general information.

Lonely Planet Norway – A fantastic, in-depth travel book with updated details on excursions, destinations, and cultural insights.

DK Eyewitness Norway – A visual-heavy guide featuring stunning photographs and maps.

Norwegian History & Culture Books

The Almost Nearly Perfect People: Behind the Myth of the Scandinavian Utopia by Michael Booth – A humorous and insightful look at Norwegian and Scandinavian society.

The Vikings: A History by Robert Ferguson – A deep dive into Viking culture and Norway's seafaring past.

Scandinavian Folklore: Trolls, Elves, and Other Mythical Beings by Johan Egerkrans – A beautifully illustrated book on Norway's myths and legends.

Books for Nature & Adventure Lovers

Norway: Land of Fjords and the Northern Lights by Rolf Stange – A stunning photography book showcasing Norway's landscapes.

Wild Guide Scandinavia: Hidden Adventures in Norway, Sweden & Denmark by William Gray – A great book for off-the-beaten-path nature experiences.

Tip: If you prefer **audiobooks**, many of these titles are available on **Audible** for listening while you travel!

Useful Apps & Websites for Norway Travel

Technology makes travel easier, and there are several **must-have apps and websites** that will help you **navigate Norway** effortlessly.

Best Apps for a Norway Cruise

Navigation & Transportation

Google Maps – Essential for finding your way around cities and fjord villages.

ENTUR – Norway's official public transport app for buses, trains, and ferries.

Norwegian Coastal Express (Hurtigruten App) – If traveling on Hurtigruten, this app provides live updates, itinerary details, and ship information.

Weather & Aurora Forecasting

Yr.no – Norway's most accurate weather app, essential for checking fjord conditions before shore excursions.

Aurora Forecast – If you're chasing the **Northern Lights**, this app helps track the best locations and times.

Language & Communication

Google Translate – Helps with Norwegian translations, though most locals speak English.

Duolingo – A great way to learn basic Norwegian phrases before your trip.

Currency & Expenses

XE Currency Converter – Helps convert Norwegian Krone (NOK) into your home currency.

Splitwise – If traveling with a group, this app makes it easy to split expenses.

Food & Dining

TheFork – Norway's version of OpenTable for restaurant reservations.

Google Reviews & TripAdvisor – Helpful for checking restaurant recommendations.

Tip: Download **offline maps** from Google Maps before arriving in Norway in case of weak Wi-Fi signals in remote fjords.

Packing Checklist & Last-Minute Essentials

Packing for a **Norwegian cruise** depends largely on the **season** and your planned activities. Here's a comprehensive packing list to ensure you're fully prepared.

Clothing & Footwear

For Summer (May–August)

Light waterproof jacket
T-shirts & long-sleeve shirts (layering is key)
Comfortable jeans or hiking pants

NORWAY CRUISE GUIDE 2025

A fleece or sweater for chilly evenings
Waterproof hiking shoes
Sunglasses & sunscreen (yes, even in Norway!)

For Spring & Autumn (April–May, September–October)

Warm layers (sweaters, thermals)
A heavier waterproof jacket
Gloves & a hat for windy fjord excursions
Sturdy walking boots

For Winter (November–March, Northern Lights Cruises)

Heavy insulated jacket (Arctic-grade)
Wool base layers
Waterproof snow boots
Thick gloves, hat, and scarf
Hand warmers (for outdoor excursions)

Tech & Gadgets

Smartphone with travel apps installed
Portable charger (outlet access may be limited on

excursions)

Camera with extra memory cards (Norway's scenery is breathtaking!)

Binoculars (great for spotting wildlife like whales and eagles)

Miscellaneous Essentials

Reusable water bottle (Norwegian tap water is some of the cleanest in the world!)

Motion sickness tablets (if you're sailing in rough waters)

A small daypack for excursions

Travel insurance documents

Copies of your passport & emergency contact info

Tip: If traveling in winter, dress in **layers** rather than one bulky jacket—it's easier to regulate body temperature that way.

Final Words: Making the Most of Your Norway Cruise

A Norwegian cruise is more than just a vacation—it's a **journey into one of the most beautiful, rugged, and**

culturally rich countries in the world. Here are some final tips to help you **make the most of every moment**:

Be Present & Enjoy the Scenery

Norway's landscapes are unlike anywhere else on Earth. Put your phone away occasionally, breathe in the crisp air, and take in the stunning fjords, waterfalls, and mountains with your own eyes.

Try Local Food & Drinks

Norway is famous for its **seafood, reindeer dishes, and traditional brown cheese**. Step outside your comfort zone and try something new—whether it's fresh **king crab in Honningsvåg** or a hearty bowl of **Fiskesuppe (Norwegian fish soup)**.

Respect Nature & Local Culture

Norway is a world leader in sustainability, and travelers should follow the **"leave no trace" principle**. Avoid littering, respect local wildlife, and be mindful of local customs—such as **not being overly loud in public places** (Norwegians value peace and quiet).

Plan for Weather Changes

Even in summer, **Norwegian weather is unpredictable**. Pack accordingly and be flexible with your plans if conditions change.

Engage with Locals

Norwegians might seem reserved at first, but they're **friendly and happy to help visitors**. A simple "Takk" (thank you) or "Hei" (hello) goes a long way.

Capture Memories, But Don't Forget to Live Them

While Norway is one of the **most photogenic places in the world**, don't let your entire trip be spent behind a camera. **Take time to simply enjoy the moment.**